The Sensei

About Yoji Fujimoto

The Aiki Dialogues - N. 10

The Sensei - About Yoji Fujimoto
Simone Chierchini, Roberto Foglietta, Ugo Montevecchi,
Roberto Travaglini

Publisher: The Ran Network
info@therannetwork.com
https://therannetwork.com

Front Cover Photo © Rafał Stasik.
Back Cover Photo © Enzo Nocera

Cover and layout design by Simone Chierchini

ISBN: 9798416362935

Imprint: Independently published on Amazon KDP

Simone Chierchini

The Sensei
About Yoji Fujimoto

The Ran Network

Contents

Introduction   7

Friendliness and Severity   11

From Cherries to the Palalido   21

Uke Is Almost More Important Than Tori   29

The Pedagogical Aspects of the Teacher-Student Relationship   35

The "Fujimoto Method"   45

Building a Physical, "Earthly" Aikidō   69

"Yukkuri! Yukkuri!"   79

'I'm Alive... It Means There's Ki'   87

Thanks Sensei!   101

Introduction

In facing this publication we have undertaken a very difficult task, that is to give life once again to the voice and works of one of the most beloved characters of international *Aikidō*. Yoji Fujimoto *sensei* has been gone for almost 10 years and has left behind thousands of students who have never stopped mourning him. Since 1971, the year of his arrival in Italy, Fujimoto sensei has dedicated his entire life and all his energy to the practice of Aikidō. In this book, some of Fujimoto sensei's senior students - Roberto Foglietta, Ugo Montevecchi, Simone Chierchini and Roberto Travaglini - have tried, within the limits of their abilities and memories, to evoke the figure and the teaching of Fujimoto sensei.

This is their brief martial curriculum:

Roberto Foglietta began practising Aikidō in 1976 in Pesaro (Italy). In the summer of 1977 he met Yoji Fujimoto sensei and began following him with growing enthusiasm, attending both his dōjō and seminars in Italy and abroad. From a certain point on he began supporting Fujimoto sensei as an assistant teacher. Following Fujimoto sensei's death in 2012, together with other senior students, he carried on his teaching legacy. He continued Fujimoto sensei's work in Russia, where he holds annual seminars as the technical director of A.R.C.A. He received the rank of 7th *dan* Aikikai in 2021. He directs the Renbukai Association with branches in Pesaro and Rimini (Italy).

Ugo Montevecchi began practising Aikidō in Rimini (Italy) in 1972. After graduating in Physical Education in 1980, the following year he moved to Milan, becoming a student of Fujimoto sensei. In 1988 he became assistant to Fujimoto sensei. In 1995, after returning to Rimini, he founded Aikidomus, his personal dōjō. In 2000 he began his teaching activity within the San Marino Aikikai under Fujimoto sensei's technical supervision. He succeeded Fujimoto sensei as technical director after Fujimoto's passing. He was awarded the rank of 6th dan Aikikai in 2013, and the title of *Shihan* in 2020. He has been a contributor to *Aikido*, a magazine published by the Italian Aikikai. He authored the manual *Ukemi - Studio e didattica delle tecniche di caduta utilizzate nell'Aikido*, and the chapter "Hand and Wrist Injuries in Aikido" in *Hand and Wrist Injuries in Combat Sports*.

Simone Chierchini began his Aikidō practice in 1972 under the guidance of Hiroshi Tada sensei at the Dojo Centrale in Rome. When Tada sensei moved back to Japan, Simone continued to train with Hideki Hosokawa ('74-'84). In 1985 he moved to Milan to study with Yoji Fujimoto ('85-'90), becoming his assistant. From 1984 to 1990 he was editor of Aikido, a periodical published by the Italian Aikikai. In 1990 he edited the Italian language publication of Aikido by Kisshomaru Ueshiba for Edizioni Mediterranee. In 1996 he moved to Ireland, where he founded and directed the Aikido Organisation of Ireland, an organisation officially recognised by the Aikikai Hombu Dojo (2001). In 2008 he was appointed 5th dan Aikikai by Hiroshi Tada. In 2021 he started Aikido Italia Network Publishing, a publishing house specialised in the dissemination of Aikidō and martial arts culture.

Roberto Travaglini has been practising Aikidō since 1979. He started in Pesaro (Italy) and soon began to attend Fujimoto's seminars, becoming his student. In 1991 he opened the Fujinami Aikido Association, his own dōjō based in Bologna. He has held courses and seminars in Italy and abroad, including South Africa and Russia. He is a Professor in Pedagogy at the University of Urbino, one of the most respected universities in Italy. He has written and edited several psycho-pedagogical essays, including *Educare con l'Aikido* (2009) and *I processi formativi dell'Aikido* (2011). He has held the rank of 6th dan Aikikai since 2010. In 2020 he was co-opted as a member of the Italian Aikikai teaching committee.

This journey into memory in the company of Fujimoto sensei's *senpai* unfolds following a number of passages from *L'Arte dell'Aikido - L'Educazione Etica ed Estetica del Maestro Fujimoto* as an outline for its main topics . This work was authored by Roberto Travaglini and published by Luni at the end of 2019.

Friendliness and Severity

Simone Chierchini - Roberto Travaglini

"Those who were familiar with Fujimoto sensei will recall his immediate friendliness mixed with a severity that required adaptation to a behavioural model very close to certain apparently rigid educational systems. I think, however, that behind the guise of rigidity lay the need to 'rectify' the student's soul in order to strengthen a certain type of bond with him, a teacher, the Teacher, a teacher not only of technique but also, and above all, of life".

[SC] "Before leaving the floor to Roberto Travaglini, who wrote the words in question, I would like to share a little story involving myself with the reader. In my opinion, it exemplifies quite well what has been said above. Towards the end of the summer of 1985 I moved from Rome, where I practised as a *shodan* at the Dojo Centrale, to Milan, to study at the Aikikai Milano Dojo Fujimoto. I was 21 years old. I took my temperament and my way of practising with me, which I had acquired on the Dojo Centrale mat. It was a very instinctive and hyper-athletic way of training, and it was totally different from what was customary at the Aikikai Milano. Once in Fujimoto sensei's dōjō, however, I undauntedly carried on with my style of practice which, as I said, was very different from the one pursued by Fujimoto sensei. Let's say that in my youthful naivety I thought I could conquer Sensei's attention through my physicality, my athleticism, my being a good *uke*...

"This went on for about a year, at the end of which I took my *nidan* test with Fujimoto sensei. The exam didn't go terribly, in fact I did perhaps better than others, but despite my efforts I didn't get promoted to second dan. I suffered a rather strong crisis, then I got over it and straightened up, because I had understood the message. Shortly after, Fujimoto sensei threw his arms open and took me under his wings. I stayed there for five years.

"So what did Fujimoto sensei do during that test? To borrow an expression he frequently used, he took my glass and threw away the water in it, water that I refused to drop on my own. He did it himself instead. From that moment on, the glass was filled with his teachings, which have brought me to where I am today. And now I will leave it to Roberto Travaglini to expand on the subject I just started."

[RT] "First of all, I would like to thank Simone for this wonderful initiative and for the challenge he has given us: to talk about a teacher who has left a mark on all of us. Indeed, he left a rather deep mark - as the word *insegnare*[1] implies - in those who would somehow seek to cross his path or enter his dōjō. As you anticipated, his very friendly nature mixed somewhat antithetically, at least in appearance, with his great severity, his need to demand the maximum from those who followed him rather closely, as happened for some of us. Certainly, getting very close to Fujimoto sensei, as you described with your anecdote above, meant getting close to a

---

[1] The Italian word for teaching, '*insegnare*', derives from the late Latin '*insignare*' 'to engrave, to imprint signs (implicitly, in the mind). Its etymology is composed of *in* and *signare*.

big flame and risking getting burned. So it was necessary to keep that *ma-ai* that is always recommended to have in any functional relational setting: to keep that right distance, sensing to approach when his will catalysed and keeping a little more distance when it was necessary to do it on the basis of his personal or teaching needs.

"It was always a learning experience, however: being close to Sensei didn't mean living the educational relationship that exists between an ordinary teacher, who passes information and the student who passively absorbs what he is told. It is something, so to speak, even more than just educating, which means drawing out - as per its etymological root[2] - what is already in the mind of the student. In my opinion it was something more, that is, it was a formative process that occurred in being close to him, willy-nilly. In some way his educational approach produced a great, profound transformation in those who had the desire to follow him and therefore to follow their own way, in reality. After all, following Fujimoto sensei, as it happens when you follow a real Master, with a capital M, simply means using - forgive me for this rather reductive term - the teacher's guidance to follow your own way. Sensei was always there, ready to put you back on the right path, which was your path.

"Often this type of teaching is in some ways very similar to what occurred in ancient Japan, or, if you like, in our European arts and crafts workshops in medieval times, if not in the Renaissance. The relationship between teacher and pupil was certainly not as formalised as the one we are used to in institutional educational contexts such as our schools. This relationship was quite different, it was something that

---

[2] From the Latin word *educāre*, intensive of *educere* 'drawing out, nurturing', composed. of *ex-* 'out' and *ducere* 'draw'.

encouraged the downsizing of ego, so that the pupil's real talented predispositions could emerge from within his soul, and not something else: in other words, it made the pupil face truth. This age-old method was then masterfully updated by Fujimoto sensei, both historically and culturally. After all, we are obviously not very familiar with the typical methods of Japanese education, especially when it is rooted in the history of medieval Japan. Yet, in my opinion, Fujimoto sensei was remarkably able to adapt this old teaching method to what all of us, Westerners, are used to."

[SC] "Indeed, one of the most remarkable things about Sensei was perhaps his ability to blend traditional teaching with a profoundly modern and open approach. Don't you think so, Roberto?"

[RT] "Absolutely, and many of us hit our heads against it. You recounted earlier what happened to you, and each of us went through it in our own way. Only the most resilient lasted. It was like resisting to the bitter end... You had to have a certain amount of strength to be able to demonstrate that you wanted to continue on your own path, which was not Fujimoto sensei's path. He functioned as our mirror. He represented a kind of involuntary Socratic γνῶθι σαυτόν [know thyself]. He put us, for better or worse, in front of ourselves, making us experience even situations of inner suffering, that's true. After all, learning the truth about oneself is not always so pleasant. Sensei had this charismatic ability to put you on your path with all the advantages but also the negative effects that this could entail. Many have fled, gone."

[SC] "True, Roberto, also because for many years now we have been living in a society that is moving in the

opposite direction. We created an overprotective society that seeks the general approval and appreciation. Sensei's path, however, was not exactly an easy one."

[RT] "I can say that I found a sort of spiritual and relational father in him. I can relate a very simple anecdote to exemplify that. I was already over 40 years old and I had never flown in my life because I didn't know if I was afraid of flying, so I had never taken a plane until that point. One day, during his traditional seminar held between Christmas and New Year's Eve, Fujimoto sensei called me. I stepped on the mat straight away and he told me: 'You are going to Pskov'. There was a moment of great confusion on my part because I didn't understand what he meant. Despite not understanding what he had just told me, I replied: 'Of course, Sensei'. After a while, I realised that I had been told to travel to Russia, to a remote place that my friend Roberto Foglietta knows well. It's a town quite distant from St Petersburg and difficult to reach: in short, it was going to be an adventure to get there, and I had to fly to St Petersburg anyway. As a result, thanks to his strongly formative imposition, I overcame my fear of flying. I got on the plane and since then I've never stopped flying. In fact, I have a great time when I do."

From Cherries
to the Palalido

Simone Chierchini - Roberto Foglietta - Ugo Montevecchi

[SC] "Let's go ahead. Actually, let's go back, because we are returning for a moment to the beginning of Fujimoto sensei's adventure in Italy. We are going to quote from '*Dalle Ciliegie al Palalido*' (From Cherries to the Palalido), an interview that Sensei gave to Gigi Borgomaneri in the early 1990s. It appeared in *Aikido*, a magazine published by the Italian Aikikai. The interviewer asked Fujimoto sensei to recount some stories that defined the beginning of his experience in Italy and he replied:

'Ah... In terms of money it was really tough. To make myself clear, I taught 3-4 times per week in a training hall, I had about 60 students, and I earned 30000 Lire, which all went towards the rent of my house. At the time, I lived with a judōka and a karateka, and there was always a constant stream of other people who stayed there. Basically, there were often 7-8 people living there. Yes, everyone shared the expenses, so to speak, but I was the only one with a real job. Nevertheless, one way or another we put food on the table: when we had some money we would buy... I don't know... 10 kg of rice. I remember that on one occasion for 5-6 days we lived only on cherries.

Another time - it was in the summer - only on watermelon... Yes, it was hard financially, but not that hard... we were young'.

[SC] "Wonderful! A constant of the age of the Aikidō pioneers in Italy, from the mid 60's onwards (this period lasted for about 10-15 years) has always been the economic hardship experienced by the protagonists of this epic, starting with Hiroshi Tada sensei. For years, Tada sensei used to live in what was pompously referred to as Rome's Dojo Centrale guest quarters. In reality, it was a small room not more than 15 square metres, which the students described as 'Tada sensei's cave'.

"The above story illustrates, without a shadow of a doubt, Fujimoto sensei's financial hardship during his first ten years of teaching in Milan, which he dismissed with his usual smile ('We were young...'). He was guaranteed some stability when the dōjō moved to its Via Lulli premises, in 1984. Hideki Hosokawa sensei, on his part, shared the same destiny as Tada sensei, in addition to sharing his lodging: for at least a couple of years, he ended up living in the aforementioned 'guest quarters', a small room without a private bathroom (he used the communal bathroom facilities in the dōjō's changing rooms), with barely an electric fire available... This went on until he moved to Sardinia.

"No one has ever heard them complain about their living conditions, or about their economic constraints. It was due to the fact that the Aikidō market was entirely new and to be developed, something that they did with tireless commitment and without breaking their word. They dedicated themselves entirely to Aikidō at a time when the word professional had never been pronounced in association with the term Aikidō. With their work and integrity they have shown the way and made possible the development of

that generation of Western teachers that in the last 15-20 years has walked with varying success the path of professionalism in Aikidō.

"Roberto Foglietta, would you like to share some of your memories of Fujimoto sensei's initial period in Milan with us?"

[RF] "I was there and so was Ugo, to whom I will pass the baton later. I remember Sensei's old cars that he had to change every now and then. He got them second-hand and therefore at some point he had to replace them. The chance of owning a new car was just an impossibility for him! It was hard moneywise, as you mentioned, but Fujimoto sensei never complained about it. He actually never even said openly he was having problems of this kind. If anything, he talked about it much, much later, when everything was over.

"The big change from this initial, pioneering period, I think it happened with the dōjō's relocation from the Ursuline Sisters hall to the Via Lulli dedicated premises, as you said. Also, in 1986, a major Aikidō event took place at the Palalido sports complex in Milan and I believe that from that moment Aikidō began to take off both in Fujimoto's dōjō and the Milanese belt. I remember that there was a big demonstration and from there on the number of students increased significantly. Do you agree, Ugo?"

[UM] "I completely agree. The IAF [International Aikidō Federation] organised its 1986 congress in Milan, and Moriteru Ueshiba, then *Waka Sensei* and now current *Doshu*, lead the attending teachers' lineup. As a result, we packed the Palalido. For that occasion, large posters were produced and put up everywhere in Milan, advertising the event so as to attract as many people as possible. Sensei gave us printed invitations to distribute to people who we thought might be interested, or at least people of a certain status. He distributed those cards based on how many 'important' people we could invite. Being from Rimini, I didn't have many friends outside of the dōjō, nobody actually, so I asked for one invitation only, to give to the headmaster of the school I worked for. I justified myself by saying: 'Sensei, she's the only important person I know…', and Fujimoto sensei answered: 'Of course, a school's headmaster is an important person'.

"This event was so successful that, as Roberto Foglietta mentioned, afterwards we received a large influx of beginners. Jokingly, we all started to say to Fujimoto sensei: 'Sensei, you should organise an event like this on an annual basis! In a short time you would have a thousand strong dōjō!' We kept talking about this and, actually, some dōjō fellows tried to persuade Fujimoto sensei to buy a dōjō of his own. It would have been to take a further step ahead, after moving from the Ursuline Sisters hall to the dōjō in Via Lulli. I remember that Walter Vergallo and Dino Ferrari worked hard to find a larger dōjō space that Fujimoto sensei could buy. The idea was to make an investment to secure a space where it would be possible to host seminars as well. That was something, as you well know, difficult to do in the Aikikai Milano dōjō: on the occasion of events like the yearly Christmas seminar we were training one on top of the other… Instead, at a certain point, Sensei decided to start holding his seminars in public structures, outside the dōjō. Anyway, going back to our topic, I remember that the Palalido event was really a turning point for our dōjō because there was a substantial increase in the number of beginners coming to practise."

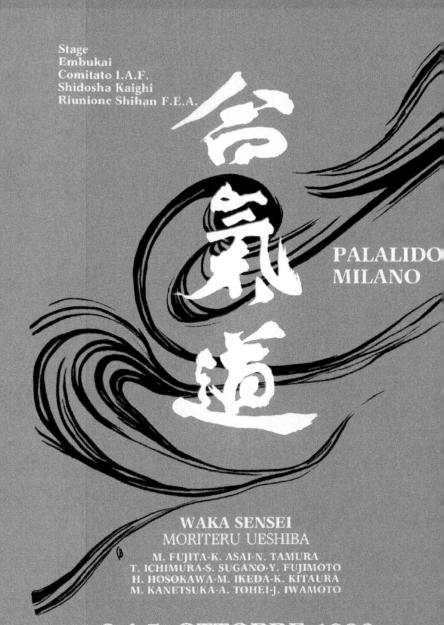

Stage
Embukai
Comitato I.A.F.
Shidosha Kaighi
Riunione Shihan F.E.A.

合氣道

PALALIDO
MILANO

WAKA SENSEI
MORITERU UESHIBA

M. FUJITA-K. ASAI-N. TAMURA
T. ICHIMURA-S. SUGANO-Y. FUJIMOTO
H. HOSOKAWA-M. IKEDA-K. KITAURA
M. KANETSUKA-A. TOHEI-J. IWAMOTO

3.4.5. OTTOBRE 1986
Aikikai d'Italia - Casella Postale 4202 - 00182 Roma Appio

Uke Is Almost More Important Than Tori

[SC] "Let's move on to practice, the topic that interests us most. Again, we are using a passage from Roberto Travaglini's book as a starting point:

'Uke is almost more important than Tori. To become strong, you have to be uke. When you are young, practice a lot as uke'.

"These are Fujimoto sensei's words and I believe that anyone who has directly studied for any length of time with Fujimoto sensei knows the truth of this statement. Roberto Foglietta, do you mind elaborating on this concept for our readers?"

[RF] "First of all, there is one thing to say, that the four of us worked intensively as *uke* with Fujimoto sensei. I think that's important, because Sensei helped you hone your timing and sensitivity, your understanding of movement and intuition of it. It's very complex work, and I think that without going through intense training as uke you can't develop as a teacher, at least at a certain level. I believe it's fundamental work. Clearly, if you start young, your body is better equipped. My feeling at the time was that I was like a piece of wood from which Sensei cut out the right shape. It wasn't just about power: in that kind of work, timing and sensitivity also had their place. There was a lot of listening. I think it's very fascinating training, and if you don't go through it, it's very difficult to develop to a high technical level. What's your take on this, Ugo?"

[UM] "Again, I wholly agree with you, Roberto, and I would also like to add that taking *ukemi* for Sensei was an excellent opportunity to learn, in the sense that instead of seeing his technique, you felt it. Learning the technique as uke was a great experience because you could feel Sensei's timing, you could feel the perfect connection that he made between the timing of your attack and his execution of the technique. You felt this power that you provided to him and that he deflected and took where he wanted, using his own power.

"Another very important lesson learned when taking ukemi was to stay decontracted. We should be able to practice Aikidō without using too much force, being instead fluid and harmonious in our movement. To feel Fujimoto sensei using his power in this correct way and not relying on force was a great opportunity, because it enabled you to stay fluid in taking ukemi. You would then try to transpose the same fluidity and relaxation in your body when you were acting as *tori*. To take ukemi for him was quite crucial, because to perceive what I described by just looking is almost impossible. Whoever had the opportunity to be uke for a great sensei like Fujimoto had a special opportunity. When you are practising in pairs, to some extent you learn the same thing, however, the experience of being Fujimoto sensei's uke was very important for me. I remember it as being every time a very productive and rewarding

experience. I'm sure you also have a few stories to tell about it Roberto…"

[RF] "When you had the opportunity and the good fortune to be his uke, it was so totalising that in some cases you didn't perceive what technique he was doing at all. I was so concentrated in listening, in being in the dynamics of his movement that after I went down and Sensei would say: 'Well, *dozo*, do it!', I would be looking at what the others were doing… because I didn't understand exactly what had happened! I will always remember this… Then I'd go looking for one of you, guys, and I'd ask: 'What did Sensei show?' This is to say how involved you were in this work of yours. It was really a very stimulating affair, one that went beyond thinking, or understanding, in my opinion."

[UM] "That is so true, Roberto. It has also happened to me a thousand times to go back to my place, after taking ukemi for Sensei, and ask someone: 'What technique did he do?' By the way, when you take on the role of uke for a teacher, by definition 3-4 people will jump on you to train together. Taking on the role of uke for Fujimoto sensei was like having a spotlight on you. Everyone wanted to practice with you and you were supposed to start: you had just received the technique as uke, and everyone expected you to practice it first; more than likely you were a *senpai* of whoever came looking for you… and regularly you would end up having to ask what technique Sensei had done! And then: 'You go first, because I haven't a clue!' It was such a classic…"

The Pedagogical Aspects of the Teacher-Student Relationship

[SC] "The experience of being uke next to a great teacher, if repeated over time, is not simply an experience of a technical nature: it is a form of imprinting, a process that does not just require learning a specific technique. Rather, it requires contact.

"This essential element leads to our next topic, that of the relationship between teacher and student. From Roberto Travaglini's book and in his words:

'[One could observe in him] a way of being that we could define at the same time traditional and innovative, a 'plural' way, to use an expression that is now fashionable in the world of human sciences.'

"Roberto, could you please explain the above, expanding on the teacher-student relationship in Fujimoto sensei's teaching system?"

[RT] "It is a very special relationship, as I mentioned earlier. As a matter of fact, I can say that I concretely understood what the expression *ishin-denshin* (from heart to heart, from mind to mind) means, even before understanding its theoretical meaning, which Sensei himself later verbally explained to me.

"Earlier, both Roberto and Ugo spoke of how they were totally involved in taking ukemi: being uke and being in relationship with Fujimoto sensei was, one might say, more or less the same thing, so much so that *his ukes*, as Sensei used to call them, were his direct disciples, if we can call them that. Through them the effective transmission of knowledge was made possible - a knowledge that was by no means theoretical, yet totally involving and transformative.

"To tie in with what was previously reported, after taking ukemi my personal feeling was that I was completely transformed with respect to how I was before. I was actually instilled with some sort of unconscious learning of what Sensei was transferring. This transfer was of a sensory or unconscious, bodily, bodily-kinesthetic nature, as perhaps a true transfer of instruction should be: something that goes through despite the fact that you are not consciously aware of what is happening.

"I would also like to add another consideration. This process of plastic transformation of the student did not take place through an imposing attitude in teaching. It was persuasive, in the sense that you happened to be in that situation and you enjoyed it. Well then, this transformative process entailed a great ability to reactivate some kind of lost plastic capacities at a bodily level as well as at a mental one. In a way, it would open your mind, your heart, your bio-energetic and bodily predispositions.

"In short, once you learned to take ukemi for Fujimoto sensei, because it was not easy, it opened up so many channels - I wouldn't know how to describe them better, or differently - that afterwards taking ukemi for other teachers who had an Aikidō approach even very different from Fujimoto's became not simple, but possible. The

predisposition to *ukeru*, that is to follow him, enlarged the field of your physical and mental possibilities, to such a degree that in the face of similar experiences with other teachers everything became possible.

"Perhaps, unlike different teaching approaches by other teachers, Fujimoto sensei's instruction focused greatly on learning how to take ukemi. This can be regarded as one of the main attributes of his great teaching skills. He placed you in front of a challenge that was basically with yourself.

"I felt turned inside-out and upside-down, and, as Roberto Foglietta also commented, after being his uke, I felt as if my state of consciousness had been altered, but in a positive sense, certainly not in a negative one. It was as if I had been recharged, and I felt transformed.

"I didn't really understand what had happened, but my body knew exactly what had occurred: so much so that later on I empirically observed a certain ease in learning the new technique that Sensei had presented. I had been shaped accordingly.

"Fujimoto sensei was very persuasive, and seductive, in the sense that he had that catalytic capacity that is typical of those who are capable to exercise mastery. He had reached such a level that he shone with his own light and you were nothing more than a planet revolving around his gravitational force. You had the pleasure of being illuminated by this sun and warmed by its presence, its physical but also spiritual closeness.

"It is something that is very difficult to describe, and that you can only begin to subject to critical reflection once you no longer have that possibility anymore, since Sensei is no longer here. Therefore now, every time I practice Aikidō, there is a nostalgic evocation, at least in my mind, because it is as if he were there.

"And he is on my *kamiza*, in the Fujinami dōjō in

Bologna. He is there, centrally positioned, in such a way that his teaching light always continues to shine.

"In general, the relationship between teacher and student is a very particular one, and Fujimoto sensei was able to exercise it on those he considered his students, provided that the students had chosen him as their teacher. This process was reciprocal and had a very powerful ascendency, which is still very evocative in me, as I imagine in you all as well - and certainly in all those who knew him well.

"I believe that for Fujimoto sensei there was a fundamental difference between his direct students and those whom he occasionally and amicably met in the various dōjō he visited.

"He had particular demands on his direct students: they had to reflect a certain type of attitude. They had to show him great respect and esteem, if not veneration, be completely available. Trust that had to be given - I'm not saying blindly, because he appreciated a critical spirit - but this trust had to be given totally, just like when taking ukemi.

"It was a total involvement, head to toe. You couldn't think 'I'm going to be uke a little bit but not really, as to be careful not to get hurt'. It was necessary to enter his movement, into the river of Aikidō produced by Fujimoto sensei's technical mastery and let yourself be transported by the current: an Aikidō *kinonagare* from which one could never escape and by which one was profoundly magnetised. It was as if he had been a great magnet, Fujimoto sensei.

"Let's also remember Sensei's vocal tone: he had a great voice, very powerful and energetic, almost baritone. It possessed a great vibration that deeply touched the physical as well as spiritual strings of our soul and body.

"It had a resonance so strong that it is still present inside

of me, as I think in many of us who have had the opportunity and the great fortune to be with him."

The "Fujimoto Method"

"For him teaching was easy. Over time he had built a very effective and functional teaching method that all his students appreciated. (...) At the end of one of his classes or seminars, most of the students (...) seemed capable of reproducing the techniques he had presented (...)."

[SC] "Would you say that it was like this, Ugo? What is your opinion regarding the 'Fujimoto Method'?"

[UM] "Absolutely. When you went to one of Fujimoto sensei's seminars, you always took something home, that's for sure. On the contrary, I have my doubts about some other teachers I see giving class around: I always wonder what a beginner can take home when they are giving class that way... Fujimoto sensei was, first of all, very generous. Moreover, he had developed an effective method, which in my opinion was a mix between the Japanese and the Italian approach.

"He himself used to say that in Japan you learn with your eyes, which means that the teacher does not explain and you have to understand what he is doing. If you are lucky enough to be his uke, you have a very privileged channel for learning - in comparison to the others. Usually, however, you learn by observing the technique, therefore firstly by grasping the movement in its globality and then focusing on the various details. Another thing he used to say is that those who can learn with their eyes are very lucky. He was alluding to the global learning method, i.e. being able to take the whole technique in one go and already start to reproduce it in its entirety, in all its movement components, which is obviously not for everyone. One must have, let's say, a certain motor intelligence to be able to do this. It means having the ability to grasp the entire technique and also having the motor skills needed to reproduce such a complex movement globally.

"However, obviously not everyone is able to do this. I have always considered myself lucky, because I managed to reproduce techniques. Maybe I couldn't replicate perfectly right away, but even when Sensei came up with something new, original, born in that moment, I was able to understand it and reproduce it fairly quickly. Afterwards, naturally, it was time to clean up the movements, refine them, perfect them.

"On the other hand, since not everyone has this ability to learn in a global way, but rather they need to analyse the movement and assemble a lot of details in order to reconstruct the big picture at a later stage, that's when Fujimoto sensei's teaching skills came into play. He gave you pointers that allowed you, even if you didn't understand anything by watching, to figure out the technique. In my opinion, this is a truly occidental approach, and one that I have seen in other teachers from the West, who focus more on their students' actual ability to learn, and continue in their learning. Otherwise it would be quite reductive, with you just showing the technique,

and then if the students understand it, good for them, and if they don't, see you next time. I am aware that once upon a time it might have been a bit like this, but Fujimoto sensei changed it by providing precise instructions.

"Another key factor (and here again I think I was really very lucky): by becoming part of that fairly small circle of students that you guys have already mentioned, the ones he recognised as his disciples, you had the extreme privilege of being corrected by Sensei. Every time it happened, I realised how fortunate I was, because during paired training he would approach me and correct something I was doing wrong. This is something that Fujimoto sensei certainly didn't do with everyone: that was mainly because the number of students he had in front of him when he gave a seminar or a standard dōjō class didn't make it possible for him to make the rounds and correct everyone. I believe, however, that above all he didn't do it with everyone because he didn't offer everyone the privilege of being considered a student who deserved to be corrected. His basic methodology was accessible to everyone, but if he recognised in a person a true, serious, constant commitment, if he saw you sweating and putting all you had in your training to progress, then you had access to this absolutely privileged channel that allowed you to receive personal corrections.

"I was really happy about this until the last time I saw Sensei when he was in San Marino as my guest, in 2011: and he was still correcting me... and this really makes me get a lump in my throat. Even though I was quite advanced in grade by then, the fact that I was still being corrected by him gave me the thrill of having so much to learn and of having the good fortune of a teacher who helped me in this. Over to you, Simone."

[SC] "I think that Fujimoto sensei was, first and foremost, a natural born teacher. This is perhaps the best possible description one can give of him. The clarity of his teaching style meant that a job that is actually extremely difficult was made simple. Anyone who teaches knows that teaching is one of the most complicated jobs there is - teaching well, of course. He did it naturally, it came to him spontaneously. I don't think he had a plan of action: when he was teaching with that level of effectiveness, he was just being himself.

"I've been practising Budo for many years, almost 50 now, and I've met many different instructors. However, I've never met another teacher who was so naturally gifted at passing on information in a simple, readable and reproducible way. That is, in the end, the task of the true teacher, if we want to define it with three simple expressions.

"As a teacher, he also had another exceptional talent: he knew how to capture the attention of his audience, so in this sense he was also a very good professional. He knew what gestures to use, what expressions to employ. Earlier, Roberto Travaglini mentioned how remarkable the tone of his voice was. He knew how to create sketches. I remember so many of them, with Sensei tying bands around his head, or knotting multiple belts together, or putting on and taking off a baseball cap... So many small scenes that basically helped him in creating an atmosphere of serious physical commitment in training, but also in keeping it within acceptable limits, that is, open, possible, pleasant. Fujimoto sensei knew how to make this system work like a perfect circle.

"He also knew when to speed up and when to slow down: that's another essential skill of a great teacher. He was never monotone, his teaching was wave-like,

practically, and he was able to respond very quickly to the mood, to the energy of the class - again in an instinctive, natural way; it's difficult to learn these things if you don't really possess them. Thus he'd masterly pick up the pace or relax the rhythm as needed. He could also teach extremely complicated exercises to those who had limited technical means to learn them. I have seen and remember very clearly that beginners and advanced students alike studied fairly complex subjects together, simply by direct observation, helped by Sensei's unbeatable pointers, some very specific indications that he presented to set certain learning mechanisms in motion.

"He had another great quality, which I tried to reproduce in my modest teaching career: he had an incredible visual memory and therefore was able to remember the students he had met in his seminars around the world. Maybe he'd meet them only once, but he remembered them. So his teaching remained *ad personam*, even though characterised by different levels of attention, as has been abundantly explained so far. It was not the supermarket-style of teaching that has become so common in the large seminars to which, unfortunately, we had to get used to with the popularisation of the Art. His still remained a personal teaching, because the people he had in front of him remained individuals even inside his mind, and he openly demonstrated it by creating this type of bond, a strong connection. It is also essential to point out that if there were different student levels, if he communicated his best to his direct students, moving from one level to another was an open possibility for anyone. He didn't have any kind of closure, the only thing he required was commitment. You had to give him all your commitment.

"Over the years, much of the above work has been

poorly described as 'power and elegance'. I find it to be quite an understatement, because yes, of course, it is true that Fujimoto sensei's has become almost proverbial. It was combined with a subtle sensitivity, as Roberto Foglietta described so well previously: Sensei's choice of timing, his touch were always of truly great quality. However, this elegance in him was in no way sought after. Those who knew him well, who were really close to him, know that he did not care at all about the opinion of others. Zero. Therefore he was never after aesthetic approval. Simply put, his action, his way of being was beautiful in itself.

"His teaching style has not always been the same, naturally, it wasn't something of a monolithic thing. Having taught for so long, the way he did it changed significantly over the years. I'd like to ask Roberto Foglietta, who has been close to Fujimoto sensei for so long, to give us an idea of the evolution of Sensei's teaching style over time."

[RF] "Thanks for the question! It's really an easy one to answer… [Laughs] It is a very difficult question, to tell the truth. I'm going to answer a little off the cuff: I believe that like all people, he too has made his own personal journey. When you were talking about the Eastern and Western methods in the educational system, I was reminded of something that he told a long time ago: 'To do things right your brain needs to be half Eastern and half Western'. Tying in with what you have all mentioned, the high value of training with him, I believe it was the result of such a process. Just now, Simone, you explained how during a class everyone, from beginner to advanced, managed to learn and practise the same movement: I believe that this depended precisely on Fujimoto sensei's ability to model these two modalities, even at thinking level, when

organising his mind. On the one hand, as we said, he presented the 'look, observe, repeat' model; on the other hand, however, he also used a by-the-numbers model, in which, if you recall, he made you try the technique individually with him counting the steps aloud, '1-2-3!' He used different systems. His innovation was precisely in having introduced, starting from a certain point, this system of fragmentation of the form, in order to offer precise tools, and decode the form as a set of very accurate movements. It had to be those, 100%, so you couldn't get them wrong: 'No, no! This way, this way', he repeated, over and over. I believe that that was the preeminent change in his teaching system, in the sense that from that point on he was able to communicate so much better with his students on a general level - I'm not talking about those closest to him.

"He managed to run seminars where whether you were an advanced student, or one of his uke, or the last of the beginners, you were still able to bring things home. I think this was the great merit of his teaching: thanks to his evolution, Fujimoto became a teacher who was more and more capable of getting his message across.

"As Simone said earlier, you're born with these things, you can't just invent them. More than anything else, I think he was a person of above-average intelligence, with an ability to reflect, reason, conceive and propose that went beyond that of ordinary people. The change in his pedagogy came about precisely when he realised that an educational system could only pass through a mechanism that the students in front of him could understand. I would like to get an opinion on all this from Roberto Travaglini, who as a specialist in the field has a privileged point of view."

[RT] "I fully agree with Roberto Foglietta's words and

also with those you expressed earlier, Simone. As a pedagogue, in relation to Fujimoto sensei's predisposition to teaching, I am inclined to use some rather technical terms, of a pedagogical nature, which are individualisation of teaching, and *forma mentis*. Let me clarify. When I approached the concept of individualisation on a pedagogical level, I was already familiar with it thanks to the fact that I had met Fujimoto sensei personally: in a certain way, I was already aware from a practical point of view of what I was trying to understand from a theoretical point of view, by reading books or listening to lecturers talking about it. I knew what was being discussed, because I had known and was still attending Fujimoto sensei, who was of an extraordinary relational ability.

"He had the ability to capture exactly what you needed, and all it took was a few sculptural words, because whatever was coming at you was said in the right way and in the right tone. As a matter of fact, at one time or another we have all been struck in some way by some 'Fujimotian' lightning bolt, which was simultaneously a bit electrifying, disturbing, but at the same time also recharging. In short, he knew how to touch the right points, he grasped what are called the cognitive styles and character motives of each individual. That's why he was able to relate to individuals in a differentiated way and in a relevant manner with regard to how the individual was likely to receive a given piece of information.

"He had great communication skills in this sense, first of all; moreover, he was also able to bring everyone, as has already been pointed out, to the same level of learning, whether they were beginners or not. This was an extraordinary talent, because it was based on a methodology that allowed everyone to achieve the same results within the same learning unit; and this is

outstanding from a pedagogical point of view.

"I would also like to add, as Simone explained, that there was a natural predisposition in him: this art of teaching came to him spontaneously because - as some people theorise today and I fully agree - intelligence is not unique but plural. There are many forms of intelligence and some of us are born with certain *formae mentis* that are stronger than others. These others naturally remain in the background, while the former become the strengths of the individual's cognitive predispositions. I am a believer in the cognitive psychology of Howard Gardner, whom I have had the pleasure of knowing personally, as well as having studied him extensively in the field of psychopedagogy. According to his theory, the theory of multiple intelligences, certain intellectual units, which are like autonomous modules acting on their own, but also in interaction with other modules, are isolable. We have linguistic intelligence, logical-mathematical intelligence, which are the only two that are appreciated in the school environment, so that if someone had a strong bodily-kinesthetic or musical intelligence, or whatever, at school he would be considered a half-wit, unfortunately.

"Fujimoto sensei, in my opinion, had a strong intelligence that Gardner isolated quite recently, in 2016, which is called pedagogical-didactic intelligence, as it happens. So it's as if Fujimoto sensei already had this intelligence naturally. It combined with interpersonal intelligence, which allows you to know other people in depth and persuade them to do what is fundamental for the achievement of a certain educational objective. I absolutely think that these two drivers, individualisation of teaching and natural predisposition to the art of teaching, were present in Fujimoto sensei's instruction.

"And then he also had another quality, which is a

tendency to perfect himself over time. Basically, from the moment I met him in 1979 until the end of his life, I saw nothing but a continuous evolution of his thought and his Aikido practice. It was remarkable how much Sensei succeeded in modifying his teaching over the course of time. It was also striking to note how, at a specific point in time, that teaching could be the only teaching in absolute. What was not true yesterday is true today and will not be true tomorrow. That's how it was with Fujimoto sensei, therefore you had to keep up to date. If you had to take an exam with him, you always had to keep abreast of his new technical proposals, because if you had performed something that was 15 years old, you risked failing.

"It simply meant that you hadn't been paying attention to what had been done in the meantime, and therefore that your mind and your body hadn't adapted plastically to the new things that were being proposed. It would have been as if you had remained fixed on something that was no longer relevant today, that no longer made sense in the present. He was also remarkable in this, in his great pursuit for perfection, that I found, especially in his very last months, almost taken, I am not saying to exaggeration, but to the highest possible levels, almost something untouchable, not reachable, at least by us, humble practitioners of Aikidō. Do you remember those last days, Roberto?"

[RF] "Yes, I do, and I also remember that we talked about it even before Fujimoto sensei became ill, as well as during his illness: it was extremely difficult to follow him, because he was constantly evolving, at such a fast pace that even though we were running at full speed, we couldn't keep up with him."

[RT] "I remember his last private classes, which were

Seminar held on the occasion of Fujimoto sensei's 8th Dan award.
He is shown here with his assistants Emilio Cardia,
Roberto Foglietta, Roberto Travaglini and Cristina Sguinzo
(Milan - 2011).

reserved for a few of his closest disciples. He did *shomenuchi shihonage* for months, studying it in all its possible aspects, but without variation. It was always the same technique, yet with thousands of different details that were actively highlighted by Sensei on each occasion and that left me dumbfounded: 'Oh, I hadn't realised that: I've been practising with you for 30 years or more, Sensei, and I hadn't noticed this. How can this be?' He'd show something never seen before, and then there was another detail that was just as new: it was something incredible. There was an astonishing, constant innovation over what was usual and known."

[UM] "In my opinion, Fujimoto sensei's great gift was that he had the ability to be clear, as he knew how to grasp what his students needed to follow him. In his infinite generosity and in his inclination to evolve Aikidō by continually modifying the various techniques - as you just mentioned, if you were doing shihonage the way it was done two years before, it was no good, you had to do it in the new way - this method of constantly modifying the technique offered you a virtually infinite range of solutions. It created a very wide base on which you could set your Aikidō in a very solid way, since you had a thousand different solutions for each single requirement.

"I think that this skill he had to synthesise what was necessary so that you could follow him was fundamentally based on his professionalism and generosity: he really made all efforts to ensure that people advanced and learned Aikidō. He was not content with 'the technique is done like this, I am a great teacher and if you learn it, fine, otherwise come back next time'. He placed you where you could follow him and if he noticed that the class was taking a wrong turn, if he saw that the students could not manage well enough what he had presented, he was capable of taking a step back. As Roberto Foglietta pointed out, he would make everyone study the movement individually, without uke, until you understood at least what *taisabaki* sequence you were supposed to apply to accomplish the technique. Afterwards you would go back to paired practice and everything would become easier. It was this analytical methodology of his in explaining a technique that made it possible for everyone to follow him."

Building a Physical, "Earthly" Aikidō

[SC] "In Fujimoto sensei's Aikidō was a matrix, one of many anyway, something we have all repeatedly heard over the years: that we should bend our knees and lower our hips. He would shout: 'Bring your hips down!' This was a basic concept through which he intended to build a physical Aikidō, an Aikidō anchored to the ground, and for this reason also 'earthly', or humble. Ugo, perhaps you could share your views on the Sensei's realisation of a 'physical' Aikidō?"

[UM] "With pleasure, I feel strongly called upon here. As we mentioned above, Fujimoto sensei has been able to change over time. When I started practising in '72, he was a lightning bolt of speed, a true ball of energy that catalysed your attention on the mat. The charm, the charisma he put into his practice... It was literally an explosion of energy. At that time I was 15 years old and it simply blew me away: I fell in love not so much with Aikidō as with Fujimoto sensei's Aikidō. That has remained my model: as they say, you can never forget your first love...

"Over time his Aikidō underwent tremendous evolution. Another thing Fujimoto sensei was good at was reading the change in the people who came to Aikidō. In the seventies there were only warriors who grew up with beatings and fresh water and people went to practice martial arts to be able to fight in the streets. In Italy we had a tradition where fascists practised Karate while communists did Judō. Then Aikidō appeared and an intermediate space opened up. Within this new space one could beat each other very hard, because at the beginning people really had a go at each other. Resisting a technique was quite normal: 'Give me a really strong *nikyo*, let's see if it really works'. Someone would regularly get their bones broken.

"Aikidō was born very physical, but then, in time, those who belonged to Aikidō changed. I remember, for example, a discussion that I had in the Aikikai Milano's office, face to face with Fujimoto sensei. I was complaining with him about the kind of people coming to the dōjō. In my opinion, they were not able to practise Aikidō because either they were not there with their heads or they were too low physically. He reproached me by saying: 'Ugo, Aikidō is for everyone, everyone must be able to do it'. This was clearly a point of view of his that had changed in time, because I can assure you that in the seventies his Aikidō was not for everyone. Fujimoto sensei was capable of modifying his perspective, because over the years he realised that a different kind of people were coming to Aikidō, and consequently a different kind of Aikidō had to be developed, one that was accessible to everyone.

"However, regardless of this, Fujimoto sensei's Aikidō always remained very physical, hence his advice to lower the hip. In short, he urged you to practice an Aikidō that was athletically sound, that allowed you to become strong or that required you to be strong to do it, put it any way you like. That was his medicine: making you practise an Aikidō that was quite complex technically, but also athletically very

engaging. It made you both on a technical level and developed the harmony in your movements, thanks to its being very elegant whilst highly challenging on a physical level. I am now going to pass the baton to Roberto Travaglini, who will evaluate this concept from a scientific-pedagogical point of view."

[RT] "I can add to Ugo's words, which I completely agree with, that the lowering of the hip was a stylistic feature of Fujimoto sensei's Aikidō. It was one of his most distinctive traits. As a matter of fact, even today we all strive to adhere to it. Personally, keeping my hip low is almost a *conditio sine qua non*[3] to be able to claim that I practice properly. Fujimoto sensei told me that one of his teachers had instructed him to lower his hip. Apparently, he wasn't doing it enough, and from that moment he lowered it in an almost extreme way. According to the Japanese mindset, you never do anything halfway. When you are doing something, you have to do it all the way. Fujimoto sensei, who was Japanese to the core, worked hard to keep his hip as low as possible, so much so that this element stuck with him.

"Anecdotes aside, behind this type of posture lies a much more complex argument. Deep down, lowering the hip means bringing the energy of the entire psychosomatic structure towards the earth, a place from which the West is rather removed, so to speak, one from which we tend to elevate ourselves. We all tend to have tight shoulders, we think a lot, our upper somatic zone is particularly on, especially tense. Thus we tend to move our centre of gravity substantially upwards, when in reality we should be moving it back to its place of origin, which we all know is the *tanden*. This is the place from which *Ki*, our psychophysical energy,

[3] Latin, a necessary condition.

originates. The more we lower our hips, the more, as the bioenergist Alexander Lowen would say, we are 'grounded'. We are humble, in its meaning deriving from the Latin term *humus*, which means earth. We are human, anchored to the earth, so much so that the term humus somehow seems to be etymologically associated with the term *homo* (Man): that is, Man is someone who is between heaven and earth, but who basically has his feet on the ground and must remain on the ground.

"You will certainly remember, Roberto, one of the instructions that came to us from the bed in which Fujimoto sensei was hospitalised and from which he would later leave us: to be humble. You will remember that he told us to be responsible, to be gentle, but also to be humble. I still feel this imperative very strongly inside me. I still hear Fujimoto sensei's strong voice that keeps telling me: 'Try to be humble, keep your feet on the ground'.

"This whole taking everything back to the ground also reminds me of how important it was for Fujimoto sensei - even during apparently extraordinary occasions - to return to the ordinariness of the technique, to normality, to the basic techniques and their simplicity. I remember that on the occasion of Fujimoto sensei's 60th birthday we had a big party and a special lesson, so to speak, because oddly enough there was nothing special about it, except that it was very normal and humble. He presented *Katatetori Aihanmi Ikkyo*, I think, then *Katatetori Gyakuhanmi Shihonage*, truly simple techniques. As if to say that - and this was his message - we had to remain centred in ourselves and not make any great flights of fancy. We should not push ourselves beyond ourselves as if we were ultra-humans, with who knows what kind of Aikidō devices. We should be simple, natural, authentic and above all in full synergy with ourselves. In short, we should remove the social mask and go back to

being who we are, with our feet on the ground, with our merits, but also with our obvious flaws: just like Sensei liked to show about himself without prejudice or fear of negative judgements from anyone - as Simone mentioned above. Sensei did not worry in the least about criticism from others, he acted on the basis of what he felt he was. So much so that several times I remember hearing him say: 'I am this way, either you take me for what I am, or you go your own way'. You are to adapt to me if you want to be with me, and that's how it was for all of us. Each of us, by mirroring ourselves in Sensei's attitude, should strive to find what he really is, beyond what we think we want to be or can be."

Yukkuri! Yukkuri!

[SC] "Another topic I would like to focus on - something that still resonates within me many many years later - was when he told me to slow down: '*Yukkuri! Yukkuri!*' (Slowly! Slowly!). At the time it bothered me a little, if I have to be honest, because not even in my dreams I contemplated slowing down, given my age. I have come to appreciate the value of this teaching over the years. We can also tackle the 'abandoning the baggage' topic, another matrix of Fujimoto sensei's Aikidō: again, I have a strong memory of how Sensei, at the end of his classes, very often recommended to forget it all, to let go of everything once training was over. Ugo, would you like to share your views on this?"

[UM] "You quoted some of Sensei's sentences that stayed with you. I'm going to contribute as well: the first that comes to mind is 'Ugo, you must go slowly! Speed only hides your flaws'. This was a kind of slap that Fujimoto sensei constantly threw at me. After receiving it, I helplessly widened my arms and continued to do as I pleased. I have always done what Hideki Hosokawa sensei suggested we did when he said: 'Take what you like, leave what you don't'. I have always learned with the utmost respect from Fujimoto sensei, but only what suited me: in terms of technique, practically almost all of it, with the exception of a few things that I have not been able to master. Not having fully understood, I am unable to convey them. The same thing applies to his character attitude, in other words, to him as a model of person or teacher, to the way he dealt with others on the mat: I took what I liked and that's it. Over to you, Foglietta."

[RF] "As for the famous 'Yukkuri! Yukkuri!', I think it was part of Sensei's methodology, as well as his way of developing an interpersonal bond. He would say 'Yukkuri! Yukkuri!' to Ugo, go slow, because you're missing out on things. He would also give each of us some other advice, so that each of us could work on our own personal message. He gave some hints to Roberto Travaglini, and something different to me, and then oddly enough he didn't want us to share what he had told us. Do you remember Roberto?"

[RT] "I remember very well, especially in the latter stages, when he was instructing us for the aftermath. He advised us not to talk to each other, not to call, because each of us was different and we had to behave as autonomous bodies - even if it was paradoxical, because he clearly wanted us to collaborate and carry on a common discourse within certain educational pathways.

"Anyway, to get back to 'Yukkuri! Yukkuri!', something that Fujimoto sensei used to repeat very often and to everyone, all of us were younger, as Simone earlier pointed out, more eager to tear each other apart physically and to tear apart the unfortunate uke who happened to practice with us. Fujimoto sensei would often come up to me and admonish me in his inimitable tone: 'Slowly, Roberto, take it easy!'

"The fact that we should forget everything is part of the

same process of 'taking it slowly', in my opinion. The two concepts are similar, because stopping and blocking the technique means questioning what has been done until then, in order to produce a change in relation to what has been previously learned. If we wish to renew ourselves, we must have the strength to break, to interrupt a technique, a movement, an idea, a thought, a bond.

"This rupture was also very visible in Fujimoto sensei's way of explaining the techniques. He was endowed with great bodily mastery, and he could suddenly interrupt the technique and present an almost photographic record of what he wanted to focus everyone's attention on at that moment. It was remarkable: you actually saw something blocked in time, almost as if it were a frozen frame in a movie. Sensei wanted us all to pay attention to it, to get the image impressed in our mind. From that image we could later draw our technical and practical lessons.

"His request to slow down reminds me a lot of Gurdjieff's stop. It is an actual technique that allows you to stop what is mechanically happening inside you. Its aim is for you to realise how mechanised your behaviour or the formation of your thoughts are. You are just acting out what is nothing more than a habit, and this habit is interrupted. The interruption, the slowing down, the reflective, self-observational attitude to grasp exactly what is happening in you becomes the prerequisite to produce change, but not a change for its own sake: we are talking about something that is undoubtedly aimed at the pertinence of the act in itself. What you are doing is not something abstract, metaphysical, but purely functional to the transformation of the situation in progress. It is an extremely pragmatic act, after all. It means to be fully in tune with the phenomenal events of the present.

"The technique is not a mechanical repetition, it is not

always the same, far from it. The uke you are working with now is indeed a different person than the one you were practising with earlier. Therefore you will have to reflectively adapt to what is happening in the completely new relationship you are having with an uke that is different from the one you were practising with previously. Your Aikidō must continually adapt and this adaptive possibility is only possible if there is an act of reflection, which in turn is possible if there is a stopping, a going slow and forgetting the past.

"After all, the past, as the word itself suggests, is gone, is no more. One can only live in the here and now, in the vital here and now of Aikidō. Aikidō is life and it is vital. If we are really to succeed in doing what so many teachers urge us to do - that is to bring Aikidō outside of the circumscribed realm of the dōjō and therefore make it become daily life - it is fundamental to associate the Aikidō spirit, the way in which we practice Aikidō, to the way in which we actively face, in a proactive and reflective way, the experience of life, in other words, of being."

'I'm Alive…
It Means There's Ki'

[SC] "Now let's move on to another subject for which we can draw inspiration from the aforementioned interview with Fujimoto sensei. To the interviewer who asks him: 'Sensei, let's talk about Ki…', plainly trying to tease him, Fujimoto sensei replies: 'Ki? What are you talking about!', laughing with gusto. When the interviewer keeps pressing him on the subject, and asks him what he thought of the relationship between Ki and daily life, Fujimoto sensei replied in his characteristic *Japaliano*:

> *'I'm alive… It means there is Ki* [another big laugh].
> *Maybe when I'm in my seventies I'll talk about Ki'.*

"Unfortunately we will never know how it could've turned out, as Sensei sadly never reached that age. However, his remark perfectly exemplifies one of his peculiarities: for years he refused, even stubbornly, to address this issue, at least on the mat. At the time I considered it to be a sign of respect towards Hiroshi Tada sensei, the Italian Aikikai technical director. Tada sensei was there, on the mat, active and proactive, and Fujimoto sensei did not feel the need to engage in certain topics which were indeed quite profusely dealt with by someone who had more knowledge in the field: *ubi maior, minor cessat*.[4] This notwithstanding, I have always felt that it was not a training component that really mattered to him. As we said before, his was a 'humble' method, big inverted commas, earthly. Fujimoto sensei's Aikidō was not 'metaphysical'. Roberto Foglietta, could you comment for us on Fujimoto sensei's attitude in relation to an element of training that is so relevant for many?"

[RF] "Unfortunately, I haven't reached the age of 70 either, so I'm having a hard time expressing the sense of Ki…" [Laughs]

[SC] "You truly are a student of Fujimoto sensei: you don't want to talk about it either!" [Everyone laughs]

[RF] "I'm going to wait to be in my seventies to talk about it. I never heard Fujimoto sensei speak of Ki. I have been to Japan several times to train, and no one has ever mentioned Ki. I believe that not only in our daily life, but particularly in Aikidō, Ki is inherent in what we do, in the technique. Why did Fujimoto sensei never theorise about it? The reason for this, in my opinion, is that there is a tendency to shift all the training emphasis on energy, on flows, and so on. As a consequence there is less focus on the technique that has to produce it. Therefore I think that Fujimoto sensei deliberately never talked about it and that he had a rather critical position on the subject. Not in a negative sense, though, but in the sense that he put the accent solely on the technique. When you start theorising, as I see some people

---

[4] From Latin, literally, "Where there is the major, the minor is neglected (or becomes negligible)"; in the presence of a more important person, the less important one loses relevance.

do, in my opinion you risk losing the technique because of all the theorising. Maybe when I'm 70 years old I'll be able to explain myself better, but today I can't do better than this…"

[SC] "Ugo, you're not 70 years old either! Do you still want to expound on the subject?"

[UM] "That's true, but I'm getting close as well… Anyway, look, I've always heard Fujimoto sensei speak of Tada sensei with extreme respect. He would always describe him as 'Tada sensei is a great teacher'. He would emphasise this publicly and then confirm it in private, because the most significant things obviously came out during the private conversations that took place in the dōjō, in the evening, when everyone had left, over a beer. When asked this kind of question, he would answer very categorically: 'To understand Ki you have to go to Tada sensei', thus underlining the fact that he did the 'dirty work'. Once he had moved to Italy, he was given the task of developing Aikidō on a technical level, full stop. Training dedicated to Ki development was left to Tada sensei. I can also confirm what Roberto Foglietta just said: in Japan, if you mention the term *Kinorenma*, everyone says, 'Ah, Tada sensei!' This is because no one else talks about Kinorenma and Ki. Would you like to add something, Simone?"

[SC] "I think it is important to draw attention to what is transpiring. In the past, people who practised exclusively within the Italian Aikikai, very often did not realise that they had received a very unique type of teaching of the highest level. I refer to the teaching of Tada sensei, naturally. What he has presented over the years on a theoretical level, and which for us was or continues to be the norm, is not so outside of the Italian Aikikai context. When I say this, I'm doing it without passing judgement.

"For decades in Italy, the Italian Aikikai practitioners have indeed enjoyed the teaching of a great master: the 'superior' teaching, so to speak, offered by a teacher of Tada sensei's depth. However, that complexity was compensated and brought back down to earth by the 'humility', if we want to use this word again, of the teaching of Hosokawa and Fujimoto sensei. Returning to what we were talking about earlier in relation to keeping one's hip low, it was certainly easy to do it at that time. There were those who helped to keep one's hip low, to go slowly, to remain grounded... Unfortunately, when it begins to be unaccompanied by being anchored to the ground, 'superior' Aikidō can become something a little odd... Roberto Travaglini, would you mind expanding the discussion on this topic?"

[RT] "Of course. With regard to keeping the hip low, I remember that a few years ago Tada sensei said: 'Those who are half my age' - I made a quick calculation and I think it was more than 40 - 'must keep their hips much lower than mine'. And he almost touched the mat with his bottom! I don't know how we could go any lower than Tada sensei, who was already a miracle... What I mean is that Tada sensei's Aikidō might be superior, but is also very concrete. His Aikido philosophy is of a practical nature, it is not metaphysical, or Kantian. It is very sensorial, very concrete. When you take ukemi for Tada sensei, you become acutely aware of this. There is something extremely physical, energetic."

[UM] "Sometimes he might even take your shoulder out, right Roberto?" [Ugo laughs]

[RT] "That's it, exactly! Everything is possible, in the sense that there is a reality, even in that instance, there is a relationship of genuine contact with the earth, which cannot be ignored. As Westerners in the broadest sense, we tend to be cerebro-centric. As was previously mentioned, we tend to shift our energy towards the head, to think a lot.

"We are too theoretical and not practical enough. This period of excessive virtualisation, dictated by the pandemic reasons that we all know too well, could accentuate this condition. In the end, we have been forced to practise less, even if I personally train Aikidō online almost every day, as it is impossible to do otherwise. [This interview was realised in April 2021, at the height of Covid-19 restrictions].

"However, mindful of the teachings of our teachers, I understand that it is necessary to practise on a concrete level, so I often train on my own. I use the method that Roberto Foglietta mentioned earlier: the type of individual practice that Fujimoto sensei used to put us through. It's a training model, just like doing preparatory work for what will come after the pandemic. Before going back to train with my practice friends, I'm reviewing my technique, perfecting it. It's a bit like being with them, but in a phase of, so to speak, preparation: like in a lab. I find that practising individually, even online, can be extremely effective, although I remain firmly anchored to Fujimoto sensei's teachings."

[UM] "May I intervene on the above, which is connected to the previous discussion on lowering the hip?"

[SC] "You're welcome to, Ugo, go ahead!"

[UM] "In my opinion, in Aikidō the hip has risen in direct proportion to the current *aikidōka* age, which has climbed, regrettably. I remember those who were teachers in the 70's and had their dōjō, and many of those are still leading the same dōjō, but they are 40-50 years older. This clearly determines the fact that they are unable to train with their hips as low as they used to. This is unless, over time, they have had the determination to continue to work hard on their bodies, so that they can still perform despite their ageing.

"To give an example, before logging on for this interview, I was feeling quite tense, because reminiscing about Sensei is something that shook me up inside. I was really emotional, so I decided to go to my dōjō and practise, to get rid of this tension. I told myself: 'I'm going to move a bit, just to burn it off', and I shot a video where I take 120 ukemi in a row. This is what I mean. If you want to continue to do the kind of Aikidō that Fujimoto sensei taught us - I mean an athletic style of training where the hips are kept low and you can move in a wide, round and harmonious way - inevitably you have to continue to work on your body. Perhaps this is an obsession of mine, or it is just my way of interpreting Aikidō: a lot of work on ukemi and on your body, because that is the base, the ground on which to place our Aikidō.

"After that, of course, we have the 'hardware' that Fujimoto sensei provided us with, and the 'super-software' that Tada sensei keeps giving us. For the outcome to be a complete one, these two components must be put together, this is evident. Everyone then will take more from one or the other, according to their personality and objective, or depending on their age. Perhaps in the past, an athletic Aikidō was the favoured, while now many are moving towards a more mentalised or philosophical Aikidō. Each one of us changes over time and therefore our Aikidō also changes; however, if the model becomes too old, Aikidō ages.

"I refer to what emerged from *L'Allievo,* the book

interview with Francesco Re,[5] who said that Aikidō in Japan is much more athletic. I felt called out by the accusation of having made Aikidō age, because I have always tried to do and continue to do a lot of work on my body. I didn't want to see my Aikidō lapse. I am not going to resign myself to intellectual Aikidō. This is what I think. Just to be clear, in spite of the many rebukes I got from Sensei on the mat, 'Slow down! Ugo, slow down!', when we would meet in front of a beer, I would tell him: 'Sensei, unfortunately I only have fun if I train like this. So either I do it my way, or I quit Aikidō'. He would laugh, shake his head and give in to my opinion."

[5] Chierchini, Simone, *L'Allievo*, 2021, Aikido Italia Network Publishing

Thanks Sensei!

[SC] "Almost 10 years have gone by since Sensei's passing. Thinking about Fujimoto sensei still stirs up a lot of feelings, as Ugo has just described. These emotions are a mixture of sometimes opposing sentiments: grief for his loss, sadness for not having made better use of the time we spent together, regret for not having taken full advantage of all the opportunities we had... But also, in essence, joy, because in any case we lived, some more than others, part of our journey together. I know that this is not an easy subject to deal with, but I would like to ask everyone to make an effort and to communicate - at least in part - the emotions that we experience when thinking of Fujimoto sensei. Let's start with Roberto Foglietta."

[RF] "Talking about Fujimoto sensei is always a very emotional thing to do. It sets in motion a whole series of memories, feelings, experiences shared not only with him, but also with all the friends and companions with whom we spent that period of our lives... It stirs up so many emotions and images, and it is truly wonderful, from a certain point of view.

"I still can't watch footage of Fujimoto sensei - I have a

whole series of tape recordings - because it really makes me feel uncomfortable, hurt. Sometimes I think about watching some of them to get some help in my studies, but I have never managed to do it yet. At a personal level, I still haven't fully processed the loss.

"What we really ought to do to honour his memory, is to practise earnestly. We have been with this person for a long time and we have all enjoyed something extraordinary, I would say unique. For instance, when Sensei fell ill, he invited Roberto Travaglini and I to support him during his seminars. It was a very tough experience, in a way, something unbelievable. We came out of those seminars looking like dazed, feverish boxers... I remember that we used to call each other: 'How are you?'. 'I'm in bed with a fever'. 'I'm also in bed with a fever'. Just to give an idea of how strong his action was. Yet I can also say this, quite frankly: I would not only do two years, I would do thirty years of that. Only to feel again his ability to pull everything out of you, to really toughen you up... and not in the sense of just making you strong. He would mould you, a bit like you were made of clay and he was bringing you out of yourself.

"I am very sorry to see that among those who studied with Fujimoto sensei there are people who are wandering in search of something, here and there, without a guiding light. This is a great regret for me. Those who had direct experience with him should work hard and not talk too much, because there is too much of it, too much gossip and criticism that serves absolutely no purpose. I'm not 70 years old, so I can't talk about Ki, but I've reached an age where I can say: 'Well, I'm going to be with the people I like. I feel good with them and I'm going to work with them. I'm not interested in all the rest."

[SC] "Which is the 'Fujimoto formula', basically. Ugo, to you."

[UM] "I would say that we should continue to transmit - and therefore emulate - his great professionalism. It was an expression, as I mentioned earlier, of his determination to make people learn and for Aikidō to grow. This great generosity he possessed manifested the mission that he felt was his own. Fujimoto sensei truly felt he had the duty to divulge high level Aikidō and to make it available to all those who came to him to learn it.

"In addition, we should try to maintain Sensei's great integrity in every way. He was a very strict teacher and his great severity in requiring precision on a technical level was reflected in how strict he was during examinations. Easy promotions with Fujimoto sensei did not exist. Either you were able to pass a test, or he would fail you three times in a row. This is what, in my opinion, we absolutely have to maintain to avoid lowering the level of Aikidō that he taught us and contributed to develop. Now it is up to us not to bring it down, at least. Hoping to raise it seems truly utopian, because, unfortunately, once you lose a key reference like his, it becomes difficult for our Aikidō to continue growing. However, let's try our best not to lose what he has given us. Let's not disperse it, by maintaining this standard of deep integrity.

"In any case, the word that comes to mind most powerfully when remembering Fujimoto sensei is 'gratitude'. Thank you Sensei! Aikidō is the path on which I have run my entire life, because it predates all the other things I have done: I began practising Aikidō before I decided to become a P.E. teacher or before I met my wife... Therefore, what I have done most in my life is Aikidō. I'm close to reaching my 50th anniversary in Aikidō - I'm one year away - and maybe we'll have a drink! In this too I am truly a 'Fujimotian'. I am not one for celebrations, I am interested in the practice. It begins and ends there, with a great sense of gratitude towards Fujimoto sensei and the good fortune of having had him as a reference."

[SC] "Thank you Ugo. Roberto Travaglini."

[RT] "I would clearly agree with what has been said so far. Above all I would like to emphasise the technical and methodological-instructional legacy that Fujimoto sensei left us: it should never remain just a memory in a film, photo or narrative. It ought to be continually re-actualised. Fujimoto sensei achieved an outstanding methodological and instructional excellence that cannot be lost. The way he taught was certainly dictated by some innate predisposition, but in some way he trained the trainers: he trained us.

"Consequently, if we really were Sensei's students, we have not only the task, but also the responsibility to keep his teaching method alive. From a pedagogical point of view - and I say this as a pedagogue - it is at the forefront, it is very advanced. His teaching method is unique, in my opinion, or at least I have never met another Japanese teacher who was able to propose something similar, or comparable to that of Fujimoto sensei.

"This method ought to be directly transmitted to the new generations, so that those who approach Aikidō can enjoy the same methodical forms of teaching that Sensei proposed to us during his 40 years in Italy, perfecting them over the course of the years. In my opinion, his professionalism, as Ugo mentioned - an ethical aspect - and the closeness that we had with him, are all aspects that should not be remembered, but kept alive through the

experience within dōjō."

[UM] "He was him and we are us, though. We are not Fujimoto."

[RT] "You're right too, Ugo, but everyone will do it in their own ways. We have been shaped - it has been repeated several times - and this must not be neglected, or forgotten. Obviously each will do that in relation to their characteristics: we cannot become a person we are not, this is logically impossible. Anything good that we have received - that is, the way of teaching a technique, analytically but also globally, all that we have brought to light in the course of this conversation must somehow be kept alive as long as possible, as far as possible and as evidently as it is possible.

"Finally, one last thing: I'm joining Ugo Montevecchi in what he said at the end of his reflection: *Arigatō gozaimashita Fujimoto sensei.*"

[SC] "We have come to the end of this commemoration of the figure of Yoji Fujimoto sensei. I hope that our highly immodest attempt to give Fujimoto sensei a voice has been appreciated by those who have read us so far. I would like to point out: this four-way interview has no other meaning except to talk about a teacher we loved. It is not exhaustive, it is not a historical or technical manual. There are many other people who could have made an equally positive contribution, and we apologise to them if the format of this exchange did not allow us to call them into question.

"I sincerely thank Roberto Foglietta, Ugo Montevecchi and Roberto Travaglini for their precious contribution in creating this volume. I am grateful to them for sharing their memories and reflections on Fujimoto sensei. I also hope that there will soon be the opportunity to meet and practise together in the name of Fujimoto sensei, something that I believe is in everyone's heart. Otherwise everything we talked about is going to remain a solipsistic exercise."

Photo Credits

Balbiano, Cristina: 13, 27, 72-1, 90, 97-1, 97-2
Bray, Declan: 37, 42
Bottoni, Paolo: 17, 31-1, 64-1, 64-2, 72-2, 93, 103, 108
Chierchini, Simone: 89
Dagmar, Ebner: 19-1, 19-2
Granone, Giovanni: 6, 20
Nocera, Enzo: 58, 81, 86, back cover
Stasik, Rafał: front cover, 15, 28, 32, 34, 38, 47, 48, 51, 60, 67, 78, 82, 85, 104, 107
Testori, Annamaria: 24, 31-2, 55, 68

Acknowledgements

I would like to sincerely thank Roberto Foglietta, Ugo Montevecchi and Roberto Travaglini for their invaluable contribution to this volume. I am grateful to them for sharing their memories and reflections on Fujimoto sensei. I also thank them for providing their images of Fujimoto sensei that have been used in this volume.

Special appreciation must be given to Roberto Travaglini for granting the use of excerpts from his book *L'Arte dell'Aikido - L'Educazione Etica ed Estetica del Maestro Fujimoto*, published in 2019 by the Luni. The inspiration we took from them was essential for the successful development of the main topics of this volume.

Sincere thanks to Rafał Stasik, Paolo Bottoni, Annamaria Testori, Cristina Balbiano, Dagmar Ebner, Declan Bray, Enzo Nocera, and Giovanni Granone for their beautiful photographs that have made this volume a pleasure to leaf through.

Finally, I would like to thank my daughter, Lorena Chierchini, for her timely proofreading of *The Sensei*.

The Ran Network full catalogue:
https://therannetwork.com

The Aiki Dialogues

1. The Phenomenologist - Interview with Ellis Amdur

2. The Translator - Interview with Christopher Li

3. The Wrestler - Interview with Rionne "Fujiwara" McAvoy

4. The Traveler - "Find Your Way" - Interview with William T. Gillespie

5. Inryoku - "The Attractive Force" - Interview with Gérard Blaize

6. The Philosopher - Interview with André Cognard

7. The Hermeticist - Interview with Paolo N. Corallini

8. The Heir - Interview with Hiroo Mochizuki

9. The Parent - Interview with Simone Chierchini

10. The Sensei - About Yoji Fujimoto

Simone Chierchini: The Phenomenologist
Interview with Ellis Amdur
The Aiki Dialogues - N. 1
Publisher: The Ran Network
https://therannetwork.com

Ellis Amdur is a renowned martial arts researcher, a teacher in two
different surviving Koryū and a former Aikidō enthusiast.
His books on Aikidō and Budō are considered unique
in that he uses his own experiences, often hair-raising or outrageous, as
illustrations of the principles
about which he writes. His opinions are also backed by solid research
and boots-on-the-ground experience.
"The Phenomenologist" is no exception to that.

Simone Chierchini: The Translator - Interview with Christopher Li
The Aiki Dialogues - N. 2
Publisher: The Ran Network
https://therannetwork.com

Christopher Li is an instructor at the Aikido Sangenkai, a non-profit
Aikidō group in Honolulu, Hawaii, on the island of Oahu. He has been
training in traditional and modern Japanese martial arts since 1981,
with more than twelve years of training while living in Japan. Chris calls
himself a "hobbyist with a specialty", however, thanks to his research
and writing he has made an important contribution to the
understanding of modern Aikidō. His views on Aikidō, its history and
future development are unconventional and often "politically incorrect"
but he's not afraid to share them. This is not a book for those unwilling
to discuss the official narrative of our art and its people.

Simone Chierchini: The Wrestler - Interview with Rionne McAvoy
The Aiki Dialogues - N. 3
Publisher: The Ran Network
https://therannetwork.com

From Taekwondo wonder kid to Karate State Champion, from Hiroshi
Tada Sensei's Gessoji Dojo to the Aikikai Hombu Dojo and Yoshiaki
Yokota sensei, Rionne "Fujiwara" McAvoy, a star in the toughest
professional wrestling league in the world, Japan, has never been one for
finding the easy way out.
In "The Wrestler", Rionne McAvoy tells his story in martial arts and
explains his strong views on Aikido, physical training and cross-training
and reveals where he wants to go with his Aikido.

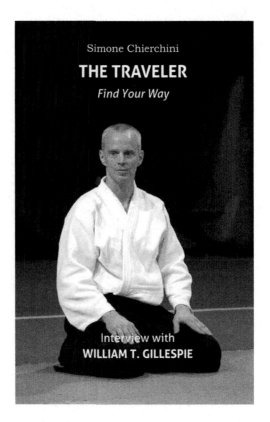

Simone Chierchini: The Traveler - Find Your Way
Interview with William T. Gillespie
The Aiki Dialogues - N. 4
Publisher: The Ran Network
https://therannetwork.com

William T. Gillespie, the author of the book "Aikido in Japan and The Way Less Traveled", is a pioneer of Aikido in China. As the sign in his first Aikido Dojo in Los Angeles read, "Not even a million dollars can buy back one minute of your life". This is why W.T. Gillespie resigned from a professional career as a trial attorney in Los Angeles, also leaving his position as an assistant instructor in Furuya sensei's dojo. He cast aside all the enviable benefits and considerable comforts of life in Southern California to move to Tokyo to devote himself to intensively study Aikido at the Aikikai World Headquarters. Currently a 6th Dan Aikikai, his martial arts adventures in Japan and beyond to South East Asia, Korea and even The People's Republic of China became a fantastic journey of self-discovery and personal development that continues to unfold.

Simone Chierchini: Inryoku - The attractive Force
Interview with Gérard Blaize
The Aiki Dialogues - N. 5
Publisher: The Ran Network
https://therannetwork.com

Gérard Blaize, the first non-Japanese Aikido expert to receive the rank of
7th dan Aikikai, spent five and a half years in Japan where he studied
Aikido at the Hombu Dōjō in Tōkyō. In 1975, he met Michio
Hikitsuchi, one of the most respected personal students of the founder
of Aikido Morihei Ueshiba, and followed his sole guidance until his
teacher's death in 2004. Hikitsuchi Sensei was a Shinto priest as well as
a high ranked martial artist; in 1957, he received from O-sensei the
Masakatsu Bo Jutsu diploma. Furthermore, in 1969 he was personally
awarded the 10th Dan rank by O-sensei.
Gérard Blaize has inherited and is still carrying the legacy
of Hikitsuchi's holistic Aikido to this day.

Simone Chierchini: The Philosopher
Interview with André Cognard
The Aiki Dialogues - N. 6
Publisher: The Ran Network
https://therannetwork.com

André Cognard is one of the most authoritative voices in contemporary international Budo. Born in 1954 in France, he approached the world of martial arts at a very young age, dedicating himself to the intensive practice of various traditional Japanese disciplines. In 1973 he met Hirokazu Kobayashi sensei, a direct disciple of O-sensei Morihei Ueshiba, a decisive event that led to his decision to devote himself exclusively to the practice and teaching of Aikido. He received the rank of 8th Dan and on the death of his mentor inherited the leadership of the international academy Kokusai Aikido Kenshukai Kobayashi Hirokazu Ryu – KAKKHR. An "itinerant" teacher, a profound connoisseur of Japan and its traditions, André Cognard brings worldwide a technique – the Aikido of his Master; a human message – Aikido at the service of all; a spiritual message – Aikido which, like Man, reconnects with itself when it simply becomes Art.

Simone Chierchini: The Hermeticist
Interview with Paolo N. Corallini
The Aiki Dialogues - N. 7
Publisher: The Ran Network
https://therannetwork.com

Paolo N. Corallini has been practising the Art of Aikido since 1969 and
during his career he has held numerous positions in this art at national
and international level. He is currently a 7th dan Aikido Shihan and the
Technical Director of Takemusu Aikido Association Italy.
Author of many conferences on Aikido and its Spirituality,
he has written 6 volumes on this martial art. A scholar of Eastern
philosophies and religions such as Taoism, Shintoism, Esoteric Buddhism
and Sufism, he loves the world of chivalric tradition in general
and the Knights Templar in particular.
In "The Hermeticist" Corallini sensei brings the reader from Iwama
and his meeting with Morihiro Saito sensei to the complex interweaving
between the different pedagogies in Aikido; from his memories of the
man Morihiro Saito to the future of Aikido and much much more,
always presenting his learned and refined approach to the sense of what
exists below the visible level of Aikido.

Adriano Amari: The Heir
Interview with Hiroo Mochizuki
The Aiki Dialogues - N. 8
Publisher: The Ran Network
https://therannetwork.com

Hiroo Mochizuki is the heir of a samurai family.
Creator of Yoseikan Budo, he is a world-renowned expert in Japanese
martial arts. Son of the famous teacher Minoru Mochizuki, who is
considered a Japanese national treasure and was also a direct student of
Jigoro Kano and Morihei Ueshiba, the successor of a line of samurai,
Hiroo Mochizuki was inspired by his forefathers combative spirit to create
Yoseikan Budo. He adapted the philosophy, pedagogy and traditional
practice of martial arts to a new modern environment, as well as to
contemporary combat techniques.
Besides practicing Mixed Martial Arts before people knew what MMA
was, Hiroo Mochizuki has one of the most impressive records in the
martial world.

Marco Rubatto

THE PARENT

Interview with
SIMONE CHIERCHINI

Marco Rubatto: The Parent
Interview with Simone Chierchini
The Aiki Dialogues - N. 9
Publisher: The Ran Network
https://therannetwork.com

Simone Chierchini did not choose Budo, he "was there".
For 50 years at the forefront and in an enviable position
in the Aikido community, he had the opportunity to witness first-hand
the major events that have accompanied the birth and development of
Aikido in Italy and Europe.
Simone began practising Aikido at the age of eight
and has travelled the world as a student and teacher of the art, changing
friends, students and occupations but never
forgetting to pack his sword, pen and camera.
A direct pupil of Hideki Hosokawa and Yoji Fujimoto,
Simone has recently founded Aikido Italia Network Publishing,
the publishing house specialising in the dissemination of
Aikido and martial arts culture that hosts this interview.

NEXT ISSUE:

The Aiki Dialogues #11

Simone Chierchini

The Teacher

Interview with
Lia Suzuki

Lia Suzuki, founder and director of Aikido Kenkyukai International USA, began her Aikido training in 1982 under William Gleason. She soon moved to Japan to train with Yoshinobu Takeda, one of Seigo Yamaguchi's most accomplished students.

She lived in Japan and trained extensively in Aikido from 1987 to 1996. At the urging of Takeda shihan, Lia sensei returned to establish dojos in the USA in 1996. She currently holds the rank of 6th dan Aikikai and travels extensively as a guest instructor, conducting Aikido seminars in dojos around the world.

Over the years, Lia sensei has dedicated her training to promoting inclusion in the world of Aikido and increasing the popularity of Aikido among young people, Gen Z and Millennials.

Since founding AKI USA in 1996, she has also led various philanthropic and social projects and initiatives.

More recently, through her work at the Virtual Dojo, she has provided Aikido teachers and students with the resources they needed to navigate the challenging times we are facing, helping them navigate and adapt to the new world of online training.

Printed in Great Britain
by Amazon